ARTS AND CRAFTS

Contents

DRIED SEEDPODS AND STALKS

Seedpod Jewellery

Collect seedpods and hollow stalks from the garden in the summer, and stand them up in a jar to dry in a warm airy spot. You will need a large darning needle to make a hole through the seedpods once they have dried. The beads in the necklaces are made from cut lengths of dried stalks. Thread them using the darning needle and decorate them with paint. Gold and brown paint have been used on these beads to accentuate the natural look. Beads painted in bright colours and decorated with glitter would make an attractive necklace.

You will need:

Selection of seedpods and stalks

Scissors

Paint

Paint-brush

Darning needle

Thread

Felt tip pens

Elastic band

Check with an adult before you pick plants and stems to dry.

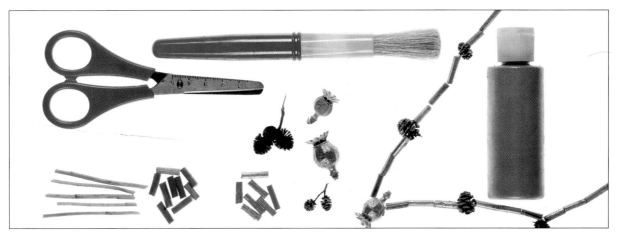

1 To make this necklace you will need a few dried hollow plant stems, some small fir-cones and seedpods. Begin by cutting the plant stems into bead-size lengths. Paint the bead lengths, fir cones and seedpods gold. When your beads are dry use the darning needle to make suitable holes through them and thread together using one seedpod to every three plant stems to make a necklace or bracelet.

2 This delicate looking necklace is made simply from some dried hollow plant stems. Once you have cut the stems into bead-sized lengths, decorate the beads using brown felt tip pens or brown paint. Thread them together using the darning needle.

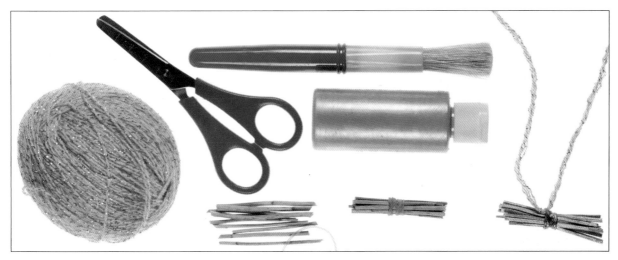

3 A small bunch of twigs is used to make this pendant. Choose straight twigs that don't have any thorns or snags. Use an elastic band to hold them together in a neat bunch to form a pendant. Paint the pendant gold; it may be necessary to give it two coats. Once the paint had dried attach a length of thread to the pendant and it is ready to wear.

Oven Bake Clay
Birdbath

This mosaic bird bath would make a good rainy day project. You could use bought miniature tiles or make your own from oven bake clay like we have. If you make your own tiles you will need to work out the number needed plus a design and colour scheme. You could take some inspiration from the colour scheme in your garden. Use a tin bowl with a wide lip or ledge for the mosaic pattern. Broken china plates can be recycled to use as mosaic decoration, but do ask an adult to assist as the edges can be quite sharp. A mosaic decorated plate would also look good as a houseplant saucer.

You will need:
Oven bake clay

Rolling pin and knife

Metal plate

Plastic gloves

Spatula

Grout

Cloth

Varnish

1 Begin by making the tiles using oven bake clay. Roll out the clay on a clean work surface with the small rolling pin. Cut square tile shapes in your chosen colours to fill the rim of the plate. Harden the tiles in the oven according to the manufacturer's instructions.

2 When the tiles are ready, make a rough plan of how you will lay them on the plate edge. You will need a metal or china soup plate with a wide raised edge. Put on the plastic gloves and use the spatula to spread a layer of tile grout across the edge of the plate.

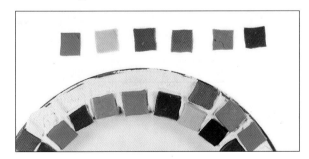

3 Press each tile gently into the grout. Leave a narrow space between each tile. You will fill this later. Make sure the tiles all lie neatly along the edge of the plate. Leave to set for 24 hours.

4 When the grout has set use the spatula to fill in with more grout between the tiles. Check that it finishes neatly at the edges and allow it 24 hours to dry.

5 You will now need a cloth to wipe off any excess grout and polish up the tiles. When the tiles look clean apply a layer of varnish to give them a shine. Let's hope the birds enjoy their new bird bath!

Dried Flowers

D rying flowers is a great hobby. Pick the flowers in summer and hang them up in an warm, dry and airy place. To prepare them for drying, remove any leaves on the stem and tie them into small bunches or they will dry unevenly. It will take up to three weeks for them to dry. You can use them in a vase or create permanent arrangements of flowers in interesting containers. Dried flowers can also be used to decorate picture frames or make table settings for special occasions.

You will need:

Florist's foam

Knife

Terracotta pot

A selection of dried flowers

Glue

Scissors

A picture frame

1 Cut the florist's foam to fit. Place it in the flowerpot and press it down well.

4 Use a little glue and place some dried flowers and a dried rose in the centre.

2 Place a row of dried lavender bunches around the edge of the pot, pressing them into the foam.

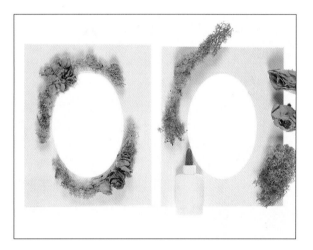

5 To make this dried flower picture frame you will need a cardboard frame, some dried moss and rosebuds. Begin by gluing the moss around the edge of the oval cut-out. Glue on the rosebuds and leave to dry. A picture frame would make an attractive gift. Offer it with a picture of you in the frame!

3 Glue an edging of dried moss around the lavender on the edge of the pot. Using scissors, trim off any long or uneven pieces of moss.

Plant Pots

D on't throw away those empty yoghurt cartons and margarine tubs, recycle them into these stylish plant pots. Create a set of matching planters for the kitchen windowsill using bright, eyecatching colours and white dots and plant them up with useful herbs. A design of white hearts or flowers would look good in the bedroom with a leafy, green plant in it, or you could follow the step-by-step instructions and paint a green planter decorated with leaves and flowers.

1 Paint on the base coat. Be sure to cover the pot completely. When it is dry check that the paint is even. You may need two coats to cover the pot well.

2 Paint a thin border at the base of the pot, then paint the rim. When this is dry, paint on the leaves in the same colour.

3 Practise painting the flowers on a sheet of rough paper before you paint them on your pot.

4 When flowers are completely dry, paint on the white and yellow centres.

5 These yellow yoghurt cartons don't need much decorating. Paint them in bright colours to grow cress in or use them for small plants.

You will need:

A selection of recycled pots and tubs

Acrylic paint in a variety of colours

Paint-brushes

Paper towel or a cloth in case of spills

Acrylic paint will not stick to the tubs and pots unless they are spotlessly clean. Wash all your recycled pots in warm soapy water and rinse them well before drying them with a clean cloth.

Cover your work surface with newspaper before you begin painting.

FOIL

Frames

Frame a special photograph in one of these pretty frames. They are made out of card from a grocery box and covered with aluminium foil. Choose a simple shape and expect a few discards while you master the method. Simple patterns are best to decorate the frames: flowers, hearts or stars for example. Have a look around the kitchen and you may find coloured foil you could recycle. The gold foil frame is made with recycled margarine tub foil! Try sprucing up an old picture frame by covering it with foil.

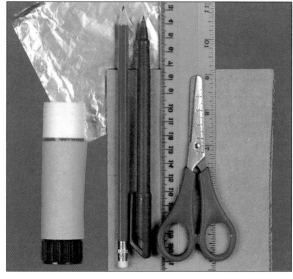

You will need:
Thick card (from a grocery box)

Ruler

Strong scissors

Foil

Glue

Pencil and ball point pen

Remember foil is made from metal and can be sharp – take care.

1 Use a photograph to measure how large the frame should be. Cut out the foil shape a few centimetres larger than the card frame.

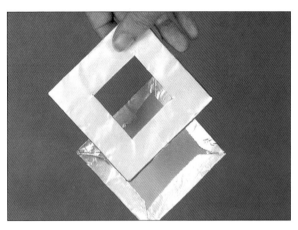

4 Attach the frame to the backing with glue on three sides, leaving an opening to slip in the photograph.

2 Spread the card frame with glue and making sure there is no glue on your fingers, gently press the foil over the frame. Tuck the edges in well, smoothing the foil carefully.

5 Use the ball point pen to mark the design onto the frame.

3 Cover the backing of the frame with foil.

Toast Racks

Brighten up the breakfast table with one of these easy to make toast racks. They are made from recycled grocery boxes and torn up strips of newspaper. Before you begin have a look around the kitchen and choose a colour and style that will match.

Some toast racks have space for butter pats and jam while others only have room for toast. When you have made one of the simple shapes you could try something a little different. A nicely made toast rack would make a good gift for a friend or neighbour.

You will need:

Card from a cardboard box

Sturdy scissors

PVA glue

Water

Torn up pieces of newspaper

Acrylic paint and brushes

1 Use card from a grocery box to cut out an oval-shaped base and four racks. You will need a pair of sturdy scissors.

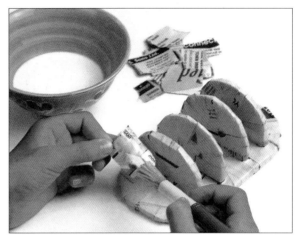

4 Mix an equal quantity of PVA (white) glue with water. Glue small torn pieces of newspaper all over your model.

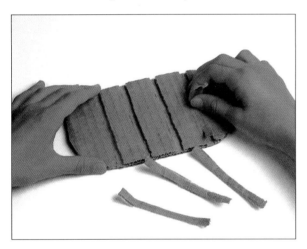

2 Use the blade of the scissors to score the card then tear out slots for the racks. Remember to leave enough space for the slices of toast between the racks.

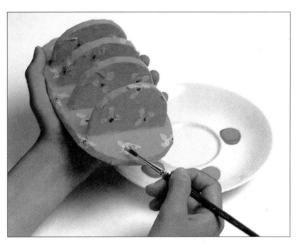

5 When the toast rack is completely dry it is ready to decorate. Use acrylic paint and a design that matches the shape of your toast rack.

Remember to protect your work surface with newspaper or a vinyl cloth.

If you don't have any glue, get an adult to help you make some. Mix two cups of water and one cup of flour in a saucepan and cook it gently, stirring all the time, until it is thick, creamy and sticky.

3 Glue the racks into place and set aside until the glue has dried.

TISSUE AND WIRE
Paper Flowers

Surprise a friend with a bunch of scarlet poppies and fantasy flowers. They are made from tissue paper and florist's wire. The poppies are made up of individual petals and look quite realistic with their black-fringed stamens. The fantasy flowers are easy to make from layers of different colours – let your imagination run riot and create a rainbow bouquet.

You will need:

Glue

Tissue paper in a variety of colours

Florist's wire

Green florist's tape

Scissors

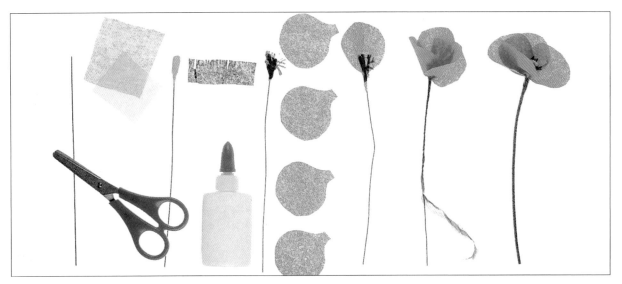

1 Glue a scrunched-up piece of tissue paper onto one end of a piece of wire, for the centre of the poppy. Now glue the square of green paper over the poppy centre. Roll the black-fringed piece around the centre of the flower to make the stamens. Glue on the petals one at a time. Bend them slightly so they look realistic. Finally, use the green tape to tidy up the base of the flower and cover the wire.

2 Fantasy flowers are made from layers of coloured flower shapes. Begin by cutting the shape for the base or sepals of the flower. Layer three colours of tissue paper together, cut out a flower shape and then cut a small hole through the centre of the papers. Wind a small piece of paper around a wire to make the flower centre. Now use glue to attach the green sepal shape and the coloured flowers. Finally use the green tape to tidy up the base of the flower and cover the wire.

Making paper flowers takes practise. Don't expect the first one to come out perfectly, so keep trying. When you get a good shape make a bunch.

Friendship Bracelets

F riendship bracelets are easier to make than you think, they just take a little time to practise. Choose several threads in strong or pastel colour combinations. Find a corner to settle down on your own where you can work without interruption and in time you will master the art and make a braid to wear and one to give to a special friend.

You will need:
Cork board or work surface

Selection of coloured thread

Sticky tape or safety pins

Scissors

1 You will need three lengths of thread. Make a knot to hold the threads together and attach the knot end to the board or work surface with sticky tape or a safety pin.

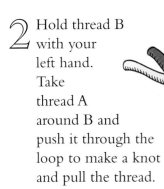

2 Hold thread B with your left hand. Take thread A around B and push it through the loop to make a knot and pull the thread.

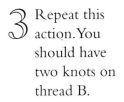

3 Repeat this action. You should have two knots on thread B.

4 Hold thread C with your left hand. Take thread A around C and through the loop to make a knot, pull the thread and then do it again. You should now have two knots on thread C. Thread A is now on the righthand side and you have completed the first row.

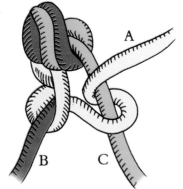

5 To start row two, make knots from left to right, knot B twice onto C, then twice onto A. For the third row, knot C twice onto A, then twice onto B.

6 Keep knotting the threads in rows until you have made a braid long enough to go round your wrist. Tie a firm knot to hold the loose ends in place.

7 Your friendship bracelet is now complete – make a double knot at each end and trim away any excess thread.

Remember to protect your work surface with newspaper or a vinyl cloth.

To make a wider braid use four, five or six threads. Make the braid as described above, knotting each thread twice, from left to right.

Brooches

Use oven bake clay to make these cheeky brooches. Glitter-spangled stars, leaping dolphins, tiny toadstools or a fat pink pig – these will all look great on a felt beret or a coat lapel. The glitter star is made from coloured clay with the glitter glued on after baking. A coat of varnish gives a good finish.

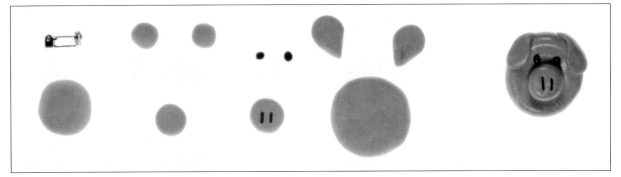

1 To make this pink pig brooch start with a disc of pink clay to make the face. The nose is made from a small cylinder shape. Use the modelling tool or a cocktail stick to mark nostrils on the nose. The ears are made from flattened tear drop shapes flapping over the face. Make two little black eyes and when all the parts are assembled, place your pig brooch on an oven tray, ready for baking.

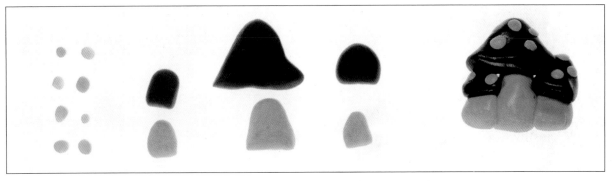

2 To make a cluster of toadstools, begin by making three stalks, one large and two small, out of yellow clay. Squash them gently together. Now make the caps from red clay and press them carefully onto the stalks. Decorate the caps with tiny yellow dots and your toadstool brooch is now ready for baking. After baking, when the clay has cooled, varnish the shapes. With an adult's help, glue on the brooch backs.

You will need:

Oven bake clay in a variety of colours

Modelling tool

Oven tray

Varnish

Brooch backs

Suitable glue

When using oven bake clay you will need to soften the clay first by moulding it between your fingers.

Follow the manufacturer's directions when baking the clay.

Always have an adult present when using the cooker.

Ask an adult for help when attaching the fastener to the brooch as you will need to use a strong glue.

Sticker Fun

Decorating writing paper is a great way to make good use of a sticker collection. Stickers come in such a wide range of colours and styles, you could customize writing paper to suit almost every hobby or lifestyle. Choose brightly coloured writing paper to decorate and find matching envelopes. Use a large sheet of paper to make a folder for holding your matching writing paper and envelopes. You will always be able to find them when you need to send a letter.

You will need:
Coloured paper

A selection of stickers

1 Choose brightly coloured writing paper to make good use of the stickers. These rainbow stickers look stylish centred at the top of the page.

2 Decorate the envelopes with a sticker on the bottom left hand corner. You could co-ordinate your paper and envelopes using two colours.

3 To make a folder to hold your decorated paper, fold up a large sheet of thin card, three-quarters the length of the card, leaving a piece to fold down into a flap.

4 Hold the sides together with colourful stickers and decorate the front of the folder with matching stickers.

Gift Boxes

Surprise your friends with one of these stylish hand made boxes. Make small boxes from paper or slightly larger boxes from thin card. A double layer of wrapping paper would make an attractive box. Use paper that suits the gift and make a box from flowery paper to hold packets of seeds or use red paper for a Valentine box. Plain paper can be decorated with stickers or coloured tape. Try decorating paper first with crayons or pencils. A set of boxes could be used to hold cake and party favours and you could personalize the boxes with your guests' names. Once you have mastered the method you will find the boxes quick and easy to make.

You will need:

Paper

Ruler

Scissors

Glue

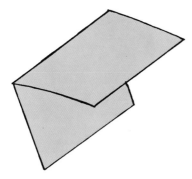

1 Fold a rectangular piece of paper in half.

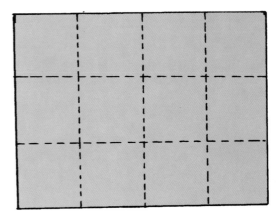

5 Now the creases should look like this.

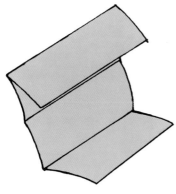

2 Fold each half in on itself, so that both ends meet in the middle.

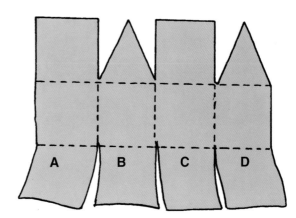

A   B   C   D

6 Cut along the crease lines and cut out the triangles as shown in the picture above.

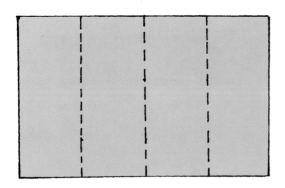

3 With the paper opened out, you will see crease marks like this.

4 Now fold the paper into thirds in the opposite direction to your first folds.

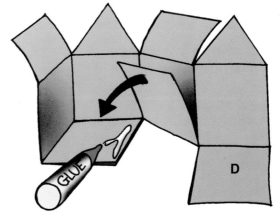

GLUE

D

7 Fold in and glue flap B onto flap A, flap C onto flap B and flap D onto flap C. Finally stick the open edge with sticky tape on the inside and make a hole at the top of both triangles for a ribbon.

DRIFTWOOD
Boats

When you go for a walk along the beach keep your eyes open for unusual items. This is called beachcombing. Driftwood is often washed up on the shore and collecting it is great fun, but what can you do with all those oddly shaped pieces of wood? Making small boats is one way of using them. The sails and flags can be cut from coloured tissue paper.

You could make a miniature fleet of small craft and feature them on a sunny windowsill. You will need your imagination to create interesting boats, masts and sails. If you want to join pieces together, you will need to use a strong glue. Driftwood often looks good left a natural colour. However it sometimes needs decorating.

You will need:

Selection of driftwood pieces

Tissue paper

Sturdy scissors

Glue

Tissue paper

Paint

Paint-brush

Emery board

1 When making driftwood boats spend a lot of time planning the best use of particular pieces of wood you may have found. Occasionally you will find one that needs just a sail or a dot of paint to turn it into an interesting craft.

Sometimes you will need to change the shape of a piece of wood; strong scissors may do. Try using an emery board or a small piece of sandpaper to shape pieces to fit neatly together. Most of all you need to enjoy being creative with your seaside materials.

When beachcombing take care you do not injure yourself. Wear beachshoes and use rubber gloves. Check found items for nails and do not touch anything you don't recognize.

SHELLS AND DRIFTWOOD
Mobiles

Beachcombing can be very rewarding: the tides wash all sorts of things up on the beach. Interesting pieces of water-smoothed driftwood and pretty shells can be turned into mobiles and hung up as a reminder of seaside days. When making a mobile you need a shapely piece of driftwood to start with. You can use thread or string to tie on attractive shells and stones. The mobile needs to be well balanced. Check this by hanging the mobile up as soon as you have a few pieces tied on, adjusting the weight as you go. Paint on a layer of varnish for a glossy look.

You will need:

Driftwood	Shells
Pebbles	Thread
Small nails	Paint-brush
Scissors	Varnish

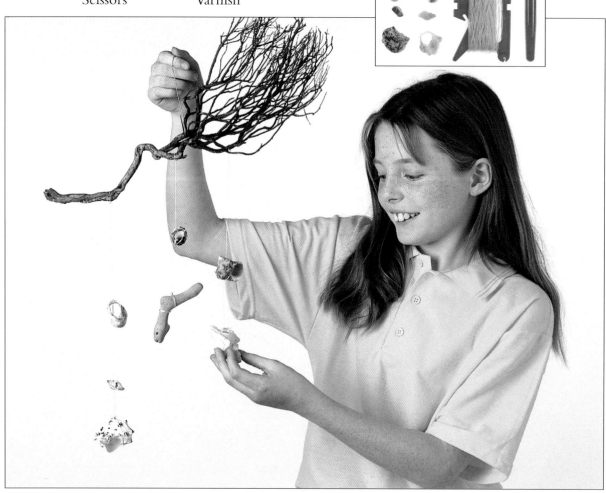

1 You will need a piece of driftwood and some small nails to make the hanger for this mobile. Use a hammer to knock the nails into position.

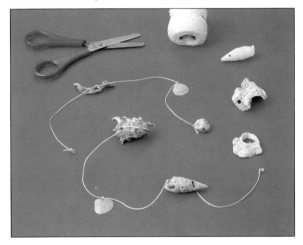

2 Tie good knots when attaching the shells and driftwood to the string. Consider how the mobile will appear when hung up when you do this.

4 This mobile is made by tying the weighted strings directly onto the driftwood. You could use loops and hang the strings on or tie them on with small tight knots. You will need to check the mobile for balance as you make it. When the mobile is complete you might want to paint on a layer of varnish to give the shells a glossy finish.

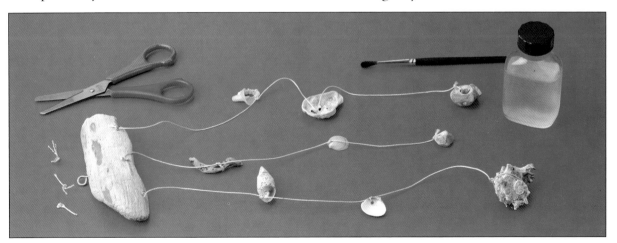

3 Once you are happy with the balance of the mobile, paint a layer of varnish onto the shells. Hang up your mobile and let it remind you of a very happy holiday.

Three-in-a-row

Three-in-a-row is a good game to both make and to play. Once you have made a board you can make a selection of counters, different sets to suit different occasions. The boards are made from card and craft wood while the counters are made from oven bake clay.

Matching shells make good counters too. To play the game you need two players. Each player takes turns placing a counter on the board. You must both try to take defensive action when it's your turn, to prevent the other player from getting three-in-a-row. The first player to get a row wins.

You will need:

Thick coloured card

Craft strip-wood

Scissors

Paint-brush

Oven bake clay

Shells

Glue

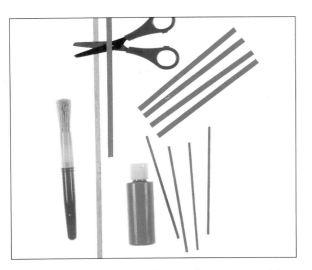

1 Begin by painting the craft strip-wood in your chosen colour. Choose a colour that co-ordinates with the thick coloured card you will use for the base of the board. Leave it until it is thoroughly dry.

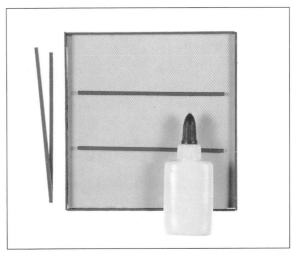

3 Attach the sides to the board with glue. Cut the board markings from thin strip-wood and glue these in place. Make sure you position them correctly on the board.

2 The size of your games board is decided by the piece of thick coloured card. This will need to be square. Cut the sides for your board to length from the craft strip-wood, using your board as a pattern.

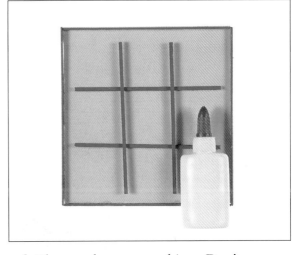

4 Glue on the cross markings. Don't worry if your paintwork gets a little scratched. Once the glue is dry you can use paint to touch up any spots that might need it.

5 These noughts and crosses counters are made from oven bake clay. Use different colours and check that the counters fit the available space on the board. Try your hand at making little boats, dolphins and starfish as a variation from flat counters.

Bottle tops
Snake

This beautiful sinuous snake can be made from bottle tops. You will need to collect a lot of bottle tops, so it may be worth asking friends to save them for you. By combining different coloured tops you could create a multi-coloured snake and if you saved only one colour of bottle tops your snake would still be dramatic. The silver shimmers and the closely fitted bottle tops give the appearance of scales when wriggled along the floor. The snake's head is made from a cork and his bright red tongue is a piece of felt, cut to shape and pushed into the cork.

You will need:

Hammer

Large nail

Piece of wood

Bottle tops

Strong string

Scissors

Cork

Glue

Paint & paint-brushes

Small piece of felt

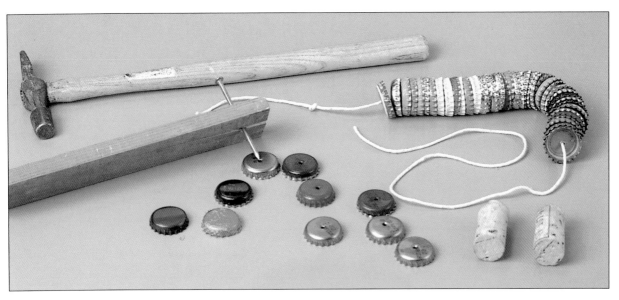

1 Hammer a nail through a piece of wood near its end. You can then hold the wood and position the nail to make the hole in the centre of the bottle top.

When all the bottle tops have holes in them thread them onto the string. Think about your colour co-ordination. A snake like this one will need approximately 70 bottle tops.

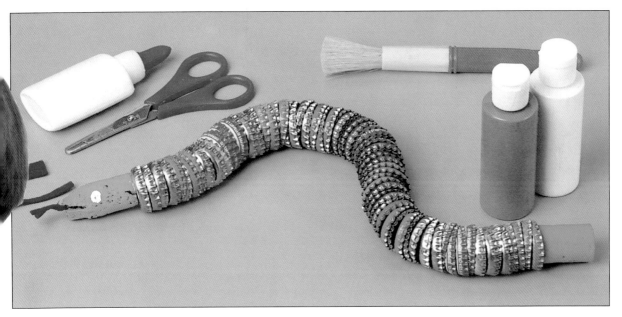

2 Attach a piece of cork to each end of the string of bottle tops. One end will be the tail – paint it green. The other end will be the head – paint this green as well and add two spots for the eyes. Cut a small piece of felt into the shape of a snake's tongue and press it into the cork with the point of the nail.

Oven Bake Clay
Pocket Pets

These cute little pets don't need feeding or cleaning out, just a little loving! The animals are made from oven bake clay, simply shaped and pressed together. Give the dog big soppy eyes by using a white flattened ball and laying a black eyespot on top of it. Place the black eyespot carefully as that is what gives them character.

The dog collar is another important item. Be sure to give your pets a tag with your telephone number on it in case they wander off! Make a water bowl and bone – and maybe a few doggy toys would be a good idea. The kennels are made from recycled milk or juice cartons. Paint them in bright colours and write your pet's name above the entrance.

You will need:
Oven bake clay

Modelling tool

Empty milk or juice carton

Scissors

Paint

Paint-brush

Large flat lid for
the cat's basket

1 To make the dog, soften the clay between your fingers then shape the body and feet. Take a small piece of dark brown clay and roll out a thin tail. Make a flattened sausage shape for the ears and lastly make the eyes and collar. Assemble your little pet and bake it in the oven according to the manufacturer's instructions.

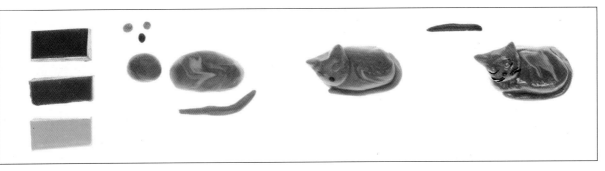

2 To make the cat you will need orange, yellow and brown clay. Roughly mix equal quantities of orange and yellow clay. Shape the body first and then the head. Use your fingertips to pinch out the ears. Roll out thin pieces of brown clay to make the cat's whiskers and eyes and position them on the face. When you are happy with the shape of your pet, bake it in the oven according to the manufacturer's instructions.

3 To make this roomy kennel you will need an empty milk or juice carton. Cut out the shape and mark the entrance. Paint the kennel in attractive colours. You might want to write your pet's name above the entrance hole.

If you don't have any oven bake clay make your pets from Plasticine.

Games Board

This neat little games board is made from thick card and a piece of narrow craft wood. You will need a little time and patience to paint the squares neatly but it is worthwhile when you consider the entertainment you will get from a home made games board. Here we show how you can make home made draughts from oven bake clay. You could use two colours of buttons or pebbles instead. Maybe you have a small set of chess pieces at home that could be used. A personalized board would make a lovely present.

You will need:

A small board-shaped piece of thick card

Paint & paint-brushes

Pencil

Ruler

Scissors

Thin piece of strip wood from a craft shop

Glue

Oven bake clay

Match box

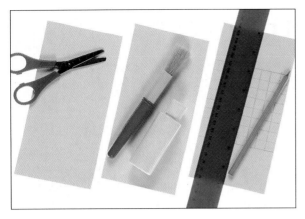

1 Paint the card in a light colour. Paint the strip wood in a darker colour. Leave to dry in a safe spot. When the paint is dry, carefully mark out the games board with eight rows of eight squares. Use the ruler to measure the squares. Leave space at each end of the board to keep pieces not in use during the game.

2 When you are satisfied with the marked areas, paint in the darker colour. When the paint is dry, use the scissors to cut the strip wood and glue into shape to form an edge around the board. Decorate the board with an attractive pattern at each end and touch up any parts of the edging that need painting.

3 Shape the draughts from oven bake clay. You will need eight counters in each colour. It is best to roll out a sausage shape of clay and cut slices to size. Bake them in the oven following the manufacturer's directions. Paint a small matchbox in the darker colour and decorate it to match your games board. Use the box to store your draughts.

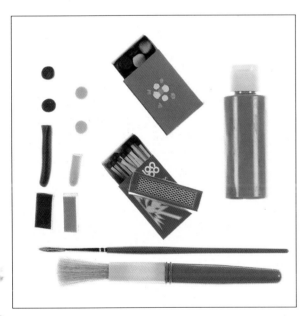

If you had an old tea tray you might want to recycle it into a games board. Ask an adult for help; you may need to sand the tray down with sandpaper first as well as decorate it using several coats of paint!

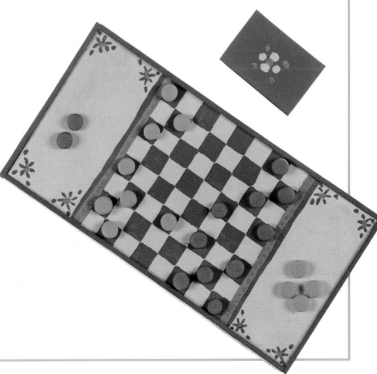

Creepy Crawly Pots

Caterpillars, ladybirds, butterflies and flowers make brilliant decorations on small clay pots. These pots are made from air hardening clay in the shape of insects and flowers and painted in summer colours. They are great fun to make. Have a look around the garden for creatures to inspire you before you begin.

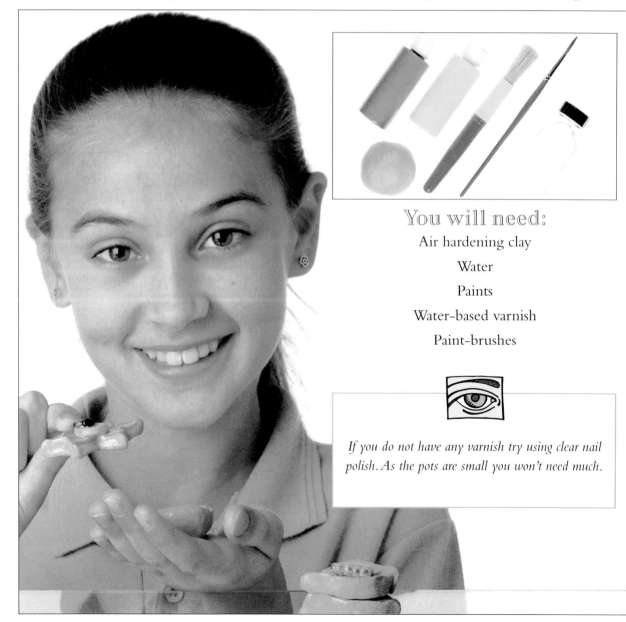

You will need:

Air hardening clay

Water

Paints

Water-based varnish

Paint-brushes

If you do not have any varnish try using clear nail polish. As the pots are small you won't need much.

1 First make the bowl of the pot, using your thumbs to shape it. Smooth the clay with your finger tips. When you are happy with the shape, make a lid to fit the bowl. Gently stretch the lid into petal shapes and make a little ladybird from two small clay balls. Use a little water to moisten the base of the ladybird before you attach it to the lid. Leave the pot in a warm airy spot to dry. When it is completely dry, paint it, allowing the paint to dry between colours. When the paint is dry, varnish your pot to give it a professional finish.

2 This ladybird pot is very easy to make. Make the base first, using your thumbs to shape it and smooth the clay with your fingertips. Make a lid to fit the base and leave the pot in a warm airy spot to dry. When it is completely dry, paint the inside and outside black. When the black is dry, paint the ladybird red, then paint on the black dots. You may need to touch up the black when it is dry.

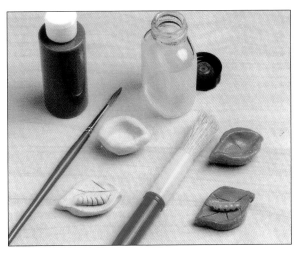

3 The caterpillar on this pot is made from small balls of clay, all joined up with water. When it is dry, decorate the caterpillar in bright colours.

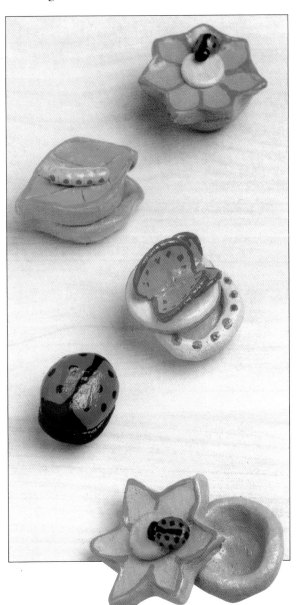

Découpage Boxes

écoupage is the art of decorating
boxes with paper cut-outs. These
boxes have been decorated with
pictures cut from wrapping paper. Old
magazines are a good source for pictures.

Use a box with a tight lid to decorate for a
gardening friend to store seeds in, or
decorate to hold special handmade
decorations for the Christmas tree.

You will need:

Boxes to decorate

Glue

Newspaper

Paint

Paint-brushes

Scissors

Pictures cut from wrapping paper

Water-based varnish

1 Make sure your chosen box is clean inside. Glue on a layer of newspaper squares to cover the box. Leave it in a warm airy spot to dry.

3 When the paint is completely dry, the box is ready to decorate. Cut carefully around the pictures, glue on the border and then the feature picture.

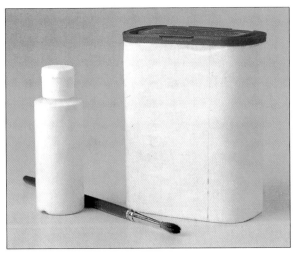

2 When the papier mâché layer is dry, paint on a base coat of colour. You may need two coats to make a good surface to decorate.

4 When the glue is set, the box is ready to varnish. It will need two coats to give it a professional finish.

Decorate small wooden boxes to use for jewelry. Clean up the wood with sandpaper first, then glue on your pictures. Apply two coats of varnish when the glue is dry.

Chinese New Year

The Chinese New Year is a time when families enjoy reunions and gifts, as with so many of the winter festivals. The story goes that once there was a bad dragon who terrorised the people. The people were very frightened but after a while they discovered that the dragon didn't like loud noises, so they all got together and made lots of loud noises. They banged saucepan lids together, shouted and let off firecrackers to frighten him away. Nowadays there is a grand dragon procession with fireworks and many people holding up a giant paper dragon. After the event families join together to eat specially prepared meals to welcome in the New Year. They give gifts of money wrapped in red envelopes to each other. The Chinese New Year begins with a new moon, and it is also the time when the farmers gave thanks for the harvest. Have fun making your own small Chinese dragon and if there are a few of you, why not make lots of dragons so you can have your own Chinese New Year procession.

You will need:

Thin card

Felt tip pens

Glitter

Glue

Scissors

Tissue paper

Paper

Sticky tape

Two sticks

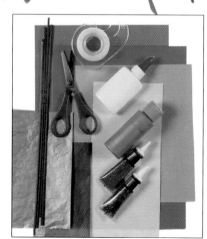

1 Draw a dragon's head onto a piece of thin card. Use felt tip pens to colour and decorate it with glitter.

4 Make the body by taking two strips of paper and folding them one over the other repeatedly to make a concertina.

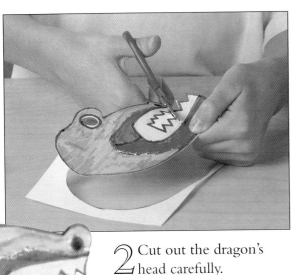

2 Cut out the dragon's head carefully.

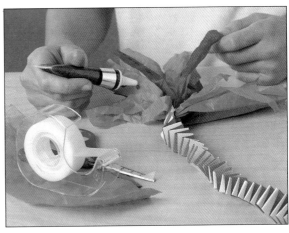

5 Attach paper ribbons to the dragon's tail. Glue the head to the other end of the body.

3 Cut strips of tissue paper to use as ribbons. Use the glue to stick these paper ribbons to the dragon's head.

6 Use sticky tape to attach the sticks to the dragon's body. One is for the head and the other for the tail.

PHOTO WALLET
Mother's Day

Make your mother this pretty photo wallet for Mother's Day. It is made with card and attractive handmade paper, but would be equally good made with decorated paper or covered with a printed fabric. A photograph of you when you were a baby would make a good cover picture rather than the cut-out flower. If you have brothers and sisters put photographs of all of you in the wallet. Use your imagination and the materials you have in your scrap box to come up with something good.

You will need:

Scissors

Paper

Card

Glue

Ribbon

Pictures

Photographs

1 You will need two equal sized pieces of thick card for the cover. Glue them onto a piece of attractive handmade paper.

4 Glue a piece of ribbon to the inside of both card cover sections. This will tie in a pretty bow to keep your wallet closed.

2 Fold the handmade paper in neatly and firmly, then glue it securely down, so that the outer edges of the two pieces of card are completely covered.

5 Stick one end of the folded page section to the inside front cover. It should cover the ribbon end too. Fix the other end of the page section to the inside back cover.

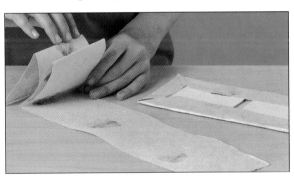

3 Now take a long piece of handmade paper and make a concertina fold. This will make the pages of the wallet.

6 Decorate the front cover with ribbon and a cut-out picture of flowers, or maybe use a picture of yourself.

Christmas Day

Home made Christmas crackers are one of the many things you can make in advance in preparation for Christmas. Fill them with paper hats, jokes (good ones!) and small gifts which you could make, such as necklaces or small brooches or badges. Paper hats are easy to make from tissue paper. You will need to fold them up small so they fit in the crackers. The snaps are available from craft shops. You might want to make a special cracker for a grandparent or friend you won't be seeing over the Christmas season. Send it to them through the post so that they can pull it while they are enjoying their Christmas dinner.

You will need:

Tissue paper, for hat and cracker

Scissors

Thin card

Sticky tape

Small gift to put inside the cracker

Snaps

Glue

Glitter

You could use the central cardboard cylinder from a roll of toilet paper to shape your crackers.

1 Before you make the cracker you will need to make a tissue paper hat. Use your own head to make a standard size hat. If you are making the hat to fit an adult–head, make it a little larger. Cut a zig-zag shape along one side, and glue the two short edges together.

2 To make the cracker you will need a sheet of tissue paper measuring 40cm x 20cm and three pieces of thin card measuring 14cm x 8cm. Add a snap, a paper hat tightly folded, and a small gift.

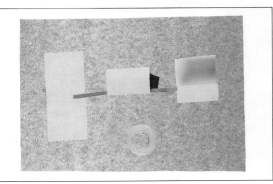

3 Roll the pieces of thin card into cylinder shapes. Hold them in place with sticky tape. Run the snap through the cylinders and place the hat and gift in the central cylinder.

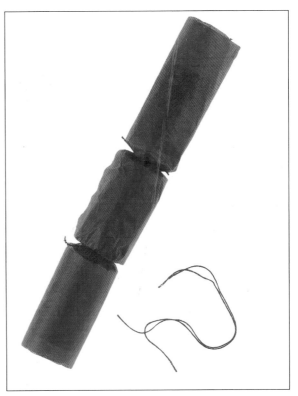

4 Roll the tissue paper around the cylinders and use thread to tie in between them. Pull up the thread firmly to create the cracker shape. Remove the two end cylinders and trim any excess paper away.

5 The cracker is ready to decorate. Use glitter and glue on a seasonal picture.

Measurements

TEMPERATURE

Fahrenheit	Centigrade
250–300	120–150
300–350	150–175
350–375	175–190
375–400	190–200
400–425	200–220

LENGTH

cm	ins
2.5	1
5	2
7.6	3
10	4
12.7	5
15	6
17.7	7
20	8
22.8	9
25.4	10

WEIGHT

oz	grams
1	30
3	75
6	175
8	250